Disclaimer

This book is designed to provide information on Basic Knowledge about Islam only. This information is provided and sold with the knowledge that the publisher and author do not offer any legal or other professional advice. In the case of a need for any such expertise consult with the appropriate professional. This book does not contain all information available on the subject. This book has not been created to be specific to any individual's or organizations' situation or needs. Every effort has been made to make this book as accurate as possible. However, there may be typographical and or content errors. Therefore, this book should serve only as a general guide and not as the ultimate source of subject information. This book contains information that might be dated and is intended only to educate and entertain. The author and publisher shall have no liability or responsibility to any person or entity regarding any loss or damage incurred, or alleged to have incurred, directly or indirectly, by the information contained in this book. You hereby agree to be bound by this disclaimer or you may return this book within the guarantee time period for a full refund.

Table of Contents

1. What is Islam? 4
2. What are the 5 pillars of Islam? 6
3. Who is Allah (SWT)? 9
4. Who are Kaffir (non- believers)? 11
5. What is Hajj? 12
6. Why do Muslim people pray 5 times a day? 13
7. What is fasting? What is the significance of fasting for Muslims? 15
8. Who are Prophets? 16
9. Who is Muhammad (PBUH)? 18
10. What is Quran? 19
11. What is the best reward of Paradise? 21
12. What are the 3 most sacred places for Muslims? 22
13. What is Ramadan? 23
14. Who is Dajjal? 25
15. Is Hijab only obligatory for women? 27
16. What is the place of women in Islam? 29
17. Is forced marriage allowed in Islam? 30
18. Is killing of a non-believer for the sake of spreading Islam allowed in Islam? 31
19. What are some intriguing and illustrative cases such as fatwas for teaching isalmic law? 32
20. What is a list of isalmic-compliant companies in which I can buy shares as a beginner? 33

21. What are the best books to read learn about islam and Islamic culture? 34
22. How should I start engaging in islam? 37
23. Should americans fear islam? 39
24. Is islam political? 40
25. Is the behavior of isis representative of the religion of islam? 41
26. What caused the rise of Islamic extremism? 43
27. Is the spread of islam dangerous? 45
28. How is life for a hindu woman converted to islam? 47
29. What are the advantages of converting to islam from Christianity? 48
30. Is nationalismun-islamic? 49
31. How did it feel to leave islam? 50
32. Is islam a race? 51
33. What distinguishes islam from Islamism? 52
34. Is islam good or bad? 53
35. Is islam and islamization a threat to india and hindus? 54
36. Is there such a thing as moderate islam? 55
37. Is islam a religion of peace? 56
38. Is music prohibited in islam? Why? 57
39. Is islam a religion that somehow makes some proportions of its followers the most violent people on earth? 59

1. What is Islam?

Islam is a complete way of life. Islam offers peace and tranquility for not just human but entire mother nature. Islam is based upon clear belief that everything has been create from GOD alone, he has no lineage. Islam is not satisfied with eastablishing the commands and teachings by Abtarctibligation and strict dictation.

Islam does not say that you should,

- believeblindly
- first believe and then know
- close your eyes and follow me

Islam takes the heart and spirit as the foundation of belief and it also explains the issues with evicence and convincing reasoning. Islam provides clear pof and tru e justification. The Islamic religion is complete for all matters of life. It is flexible because it is close to the human nature. There is no Muslim who does not no the signs of truth. The Universe guides them to the oneness of God Almighty.

Islam is the fastest growing religion in the world todays, because,

- Islam conforms to human requirements and needs
- Islam can develop without any decay over the centuries
- Islam keeps it complete strength of life and felxivility
- Islam is the religion that gave the world the most established and affirmed legislations

Islam is not forced upon people, it is for them who can submit themselves truly from their heart and their action would follow once they submit soulheartedly in the religion. Once they find solance in the oneness of God, everything that Islam called obligatory comes automatically for the person to perform. Discover Islam in your own terms, no need to feel pressured by any community.

2. What are the 5 pillars of Islam?

The 5 pillars of Islam are the fundamentals of being a Muslim. Without these things one cannot be considered as Muslim. Theyarelistedbelow in order,

    a. The Testimony of Faith:

The ultimate testimony of Islamic faith is uttering the Shahadah and believing it from the heart. Shahadah is, "La ilahailla Allah, Muhammadurrasoolu Allah."

Meaning, "There is no true god (deity) but God (Allah), and Muhammad is the Messenger (Prophet) of God."

Here one is acknowledging that there is no other deity exist than Allah and he alone should be worshipped. The second part is acknowledging that Muhammad (PBUH) is the last messenger of Allah. This is in the first order because without this faith, every other act of worshipping Allah is pointless.

    b. Prayer

The Muslims are obligated to pray 5 times a day, these prayers are, Fajr, Dhuhr, Ashr, Maghrib, Esha. Each prayer has its own significance. The timings of these prayers are also different. Anyone can ask "Why does Allah need prayers from human?,, The answer is quite simple, Allah does not need our prayers, we need Allah's mercy and through prayers one can establish direct link with the supreme God. Prayergivestranquilityto the mind and soul.

c. Zakat (Charity)

In every Ramadan (The month of fasting), before EidUlFitr Muslims have to pay Zakat (give charity) to the ones that are in need. This act of worship increases the wealth of the payer and also improves the condition of a poor person. Muslims have to give only a percentage of their property, and Zakat is not obligatory on everyone. Only if someone possesses 85 g gold or belongings that is equivalent to that sum is obligated to pay zakat.

d. Fasting

Fasting in the 9th month (Ramadan) is obligatory for every Muslim. They have to fast for 29-30 days depending on the moon. Fasting means, *staying sway* and it does not refer to refraining from food alone, it also implies that while fasting one should stay away from backbiting, lying, cursing, fighting etc. It is a month of purification of the body and soul.

e. Hajj (Pilgrimage)

Annual Pilgrimage to Makkah during the month of Dhul-Hijjah is obligatory upon every Muslim if they are financially sufficient to perform it. They need to perform Hajj at least once in their lifetime.

3. Who is Allah (SWT)?

The Almighty creator is the All knowing, He is the fully-aware of the creation of humans, He is the all-knowing of what happened in past, present and future. Knowing the creator is the ultimate goal of our life.

Allah does not need humans, or their prayers, it is human beings who are lost without the guidance of Allah. He created us from dirt and after death we all shall go in the dirt (grave). With His commandments, we shall ressurect again.

Allah is known by 99 names, some of them are Ar Rahman (The All-Compassionate), As-Salam (The source of Peace), Al-Muhaymin (The Guardian), Al-Ghaffar (All Forgiving), Al-Basit (The Reliever), As-Sami (The Hearer of All) etc.

Photo credit

Narrated Abu Musa Al-Ashari: The Prophet said, "None is more patient than Allah against the harmful and annoying words He hears (from the people): They ascribe children to Him, yet He bestows upon them health and provision .

Narrated Ibn Umar: The Prophet said, "The keys of the unseen are five and none knows them but Allah: (1) None knows what is in the womb, but Allah: (2) None knows what will happen tomorrow, but Allah; (3) None knows when it will rain, but Allah; (4) None knows where he will die, but Allah (knows that); (5) and none knows when the Hour will be established, but Allah."

4. Who are Kaffir (non- believers)?

The kaffir, the non-belivers are the one who rejects Islam, Allah and the messenger Muhammad (PBUH). Anyone who does not believe in Allah and His oneness is considered a non-believer. Allah has immense mercy for the mankind. Even if someone faces Him with a mountain filled with sins, He would forgive them if they repent sincerely when they were given time in the earth. But Allah has no mercy for a non-believer who never accepted that Allah is the supreme governing party and alone He is worthy of worship.

There are several references in the Quran that establishes how poorly a non-believer would be treated in the after-life.

The punishment of those who wage war (against) Allah and His Messenger and strive in the earth spreading corruption (is) that they be killed or they be crucified or be cut off their hands and their feet of opposite sides or they be exiled from the land. That (is) for them disgrace in the world and for them in the Hereafter (is) a punishment great. (Al Mayidah 5:33)

5. What is Hajj?

Hajj or pilgrimage is one of the pillars/foundation of Islam. Every year in the Islamic month of Dhul-Hajj Muslims living all over the world unite in Makkah, Saudi Arabia. They perform the pilgrimage which is 9 days long.

Any Muslim who can finance the costing of making the pilgrimage must go for it at least once in their life. Some Muslims go to perform Hajj several times.

The process is quite elaborated.

6. Why do Muslim people pray 5 times a day?

Muslims pray 5 times a day because it was obligated by God that no matter in which condition they are in, they must offer the 5 daily prayers. To offer the prayer, one has to stand up and Allah has given commandments that if a person if unable to stand he may sit and offer the prayer. If a person is unable to sit even then they should not skip the prayer, they have the liberty of offering it whilest they are lying down.

'Imraan ibn Husayn (may Allaah be pleased with him) who said: I had haemorrhoids, and I asked the Prophet (peace and blessings of Allah be upon him) about praying. He said: "Pray standing; if you cannot, then sitting; and if you cannot, then lying on your side." [Al Bukhari-1050]

Ibn Qudaamah (may Allah have mercy on him) said: If standing will make a sick person's sickness worse, then he should pray sitting. The scholars are unanimously agreed that a person who cannot stand may pray sitting. The Prophet (peace and blessings of Allah be upon him) said to 'Imraan ibn Husayn: "Pray standing; if you cannot, then sitting; and if you cannot, then lying on your side."

The 5 daily prayers are,

- Fajr (which is prayed 1 hour before the sunrise)
- Dhuhr (which is prayed when the sun is right above the head)
- Ashr (which is prayed 2 hours before the sunset)
- Maghrib (which is prayed right after the sunset)
- Esha (which is prayer 1.5-2 hours after the sunset)

In order to offer the prayers Muslims have to do ablution which is the act of cleaning oneself.

There is a time when Muslims are forbidden to offer prayer, it is during the sunrise. It was commanded in order to proof that Muslims are not worshipping the sun rather they are worshipping the creator who create the sun and everything else.

7. What is fasting? What is the significance of fasting for Muslims?

Fasting in the arabic form is shawom, which mean refraining from or staying away. A fallacy is prevalent among not only non-muslims but also muslims that fasting means avoiding food intake between the sunrise and sunset, but in actuality fasting is much more than that.

Fasting is refraining oneself from fighting, backbiting, lying, fornicating. It is an overall attempt to purify oneself and be productive. You not only purify your body but you work hard to purify your soul. The soul is deprived from nurturing, we take care of our body and forget that soul is what needs most nurturing.

It is obligatory for Muslims to fast the whole month of Ramadan (the 9th month of Islamic calender). Muslims also fast all through the year and different days have different significance for fasting. There are 5 days which are prohibited to fast, these are,

On Eid Al Fitr

On Eid Al Azha

The three days following Eid Al Azha

"O you who believe! Fasting is prescribed for you, as it was prescribed for those who came before you; that you will perhaps be God-fearing." [Al-Qur'an 2:183]

8. Who are Prophets?

Prophets are the savior of mankind, they were sent from Allah time to time. The first prophet and human to ever walk on the earth was Adam (AS) and the last prophet is Muhammad (PBUH). In arabic language there are two words that define prophets, Nabi and Rasool. Nabitranstales into prophet and rasool translates in messenger in English.

There are 25 prophets who were mentions in the Holy book of Quran. Below is a list of the prophets, the similarities with the prophets in Quran and Bible is uncanny.

Adam (AS)
Idris (As)/(Enoch)
Nuh (As)/ (Noah)
Hud (As)/ (Heber)
Salih (As)/ (Methusaleh)
Lut (As)/ (Lot)
Ibrahim (As)/ (Abraham)
Ismail (As)/ (Ishmael)
Ishaq (As)/ (Isaac)
Yaqub (As)/ (Jacob)
Yusuf (As)/ (Joseph)
Shu'aib (As)/ (Jethro)
Ayyub (As)/ (Job)
Dhulkifl (As)/ (Ezekiel)
Musa (As)/ (Moses)
Harun (As)/ (Aaron)
Dawud (As)/ (David)
Sulayman (As)/ (Solomon)
Ilias (As)/ (Elias)

Alyasa (As)/ (Elisha)
Yunus (As)/ (Jonah)
Zakariya (As)/ (Zachariah)
Yahya (As)/ (John the Baptist)
Isa (As)/ (Jesus)
Muhammad (PBUH)

Each prophet had a mission and they tried their best to spread the light of Islam and the commandments of Allah. Some of the prophets were also given special power to make their mission more feasible.

9. Who is Muhammad (PBUH)?

Muhammad (PBUH) is a nabi and the last messenger from Allah. Before him there were 24 prophets who came on earth and spread Islam and Allah's commandments. After Muhammad (PBUH) no prophets would come from Allah.

He was born in 570 in Makkah. His father couldn't see him and he was unfortunate enough to lose his mother at the age of 6. He was brought up by his uncle Abu Talib who died as a non-believer of Islam. It shows that prophets who not have the power to turn hearts, only seer will of a person and God's will can turn hearts.

The quranic verses (the revealation) came to him when he was 40 and it continued for about 23 years.

All through Muhammad's life he faced so many tribulations, battles, lost so many of his family members and companions, but nothing stood in his way of spreading Islam. His soul goal was to show the path of righteousness to his Ummah (The entire Muslims who were to born after the death of Muhammad (PBUH).

He is the only prophet who loved his ummah more than he loved his companions. He loved us so much that on the day of Judgement, he is the only prophet who would suplicate to Allah for us.

He was and still is the embodiment of honestly, loyalty, sincerity for not just muslims but for non-believers too. That is why people like Mahatma Gandhi, Sir George Bernard Shaw, Thomas Carlyle, W. Montgomery Watt, Dr. William Draper, Leo Tolstoy said words favoring him.

10. What is Quran?

The Quran is the holy book that came down from Allah to give eternal guidance to the entire humanity. The Quran was revealed to give guidance to the humanity and still continues to lead the Muslims in their wordly life and their path to afterlife.

In different countries and civilization, it is still the same exactly as it was revealed.

There is a saying, if you want to speak to Allah, say your prayers and if you want Allah to speak to you, read Quran because Quran uploads Allah's messege.

The Quran Eastablishes proofs about,

- the matter of divinity from the universe
- thespirit
- the history of the existence of God
- His onenessandcompleteness
- Resurrection
- The protential of creating humans
- Creating the heavens and the earth and reviving the land after her death
- God'swisdomthroughjustice
- Rewarding the good doer and punishing the bad doer

Quran consists of 114 surahs and the first revealation of the quran was from chapter 96,

"Read, in the name of thy Lord, Who created?

Created man, out of a clot (embryo).

Proclaim! And thy Lord is Most Bountiful,

He Who taught the use of the pen?

Taught man that which he knew not.

Nay, but man doth transgress all bounds,

In that he looketh upon himself as self-sufficient.

Verily, to thy Lord is the return (of all)."

11. What is the best reward of Paradise?

There are many rewards a muslim would get in paradise. From getting 70 angels as their mistresses, a mansion that he dreamt of, a river flowing beside the mansion. They would get trees filled with amazing fruits, the taste of those fruits can incomparable to anything they have ever tasted on this earth. They would get garments made of silk and the quantity has no limit. They would get servants, batlers who would be always ready to fulfill his commands. They would also be able to drink from the pond of Muhammad (PBUH) which is a blessing for those who belief.

Everything that were forbidden in this world would be permitted in paradise. There would be no sins, jealousy, greed, crushing or fighting. Peace would prevail in the air.

Amongst all these, the greatest reward of paradise is still being able to glance at the one who created you. You would be able to look directly at your creator.

The Prophet sallallahualayhiwasallam said:

"When those deserving of Paradise would enter Paradise, the Blessed and the Exalted would ask: Do you wish Me to give you anything more? They would say: Hast Thou not brightened our faces? Hast Thou not made us enter Paradise and saved us from Fire? He (the narrator) said. He (Allah) would lift the veil, and of things given to them nothing would be dearer to them than the sight of their Lord, the Mighty and the Glorious. He then recited the verse: {For those who do good is the best reward and even more} "

[Sahih Muslim]

12. What are the 3 most sacred places for Muslims?

The whole earth is precious to a muslim because every where he looks, he finds Allah's creation and architural beauty. But certain places have more significance over others.

First to come on the list is the Makkah. It is needless to say how valueableKabah is for every Muslim and every muslim who cannot afford to visit kabah in person, they long to visit it and ask Allah for the blessing one day. It is situated in Saudi Arabia. The kabah was built around a black stone by Ibrahim (AS) by the commandments of Allah. Since then muslims pray their prayers in the direction of Kabah. People pray in Mashjid Al Haram in Makkah.

The second sacred place for muslims is the city of Madinah. It is also called the City of Muhammad. Madinah was very precious for Muhammad (PBUH) and it is there he found his first followers. People pray in Mashjid Al Nababi in Madinah.

The thrid place is Jerusalem, Palestine. Mashjid Al Aqsa was the first Kabah for Muslims. They used to offer prayers facing to that direction, later commandments came from Allah that Kabah in Makkah should be followed for praying. This place is so important in the Islamic history is because Muhammad (PBUH) was brought here from Makkah in one night and from there he went to the heaven and hell in that same night. The jounrey was called Al Isra al Miraj.

13. What is Ramadan?

As mentioned earlier Ramadan is the 9th month of the Islamic Calender and in this month muslims fast for the entire month. The month long fasting comes to an end with the celebration of Eid Al Fitr. The significance of fasting is already mentioned earlier, so I would not reiterate the same fact but there are more to the month of Ramadan. For instance, Muslims get 10 to 700 times reward for each good deed they perform.

It is proven in the hadith that Abu Hurayrah (may Allah be pleased with him) said: The Messenger of Allah (blessings and peace of Allah be upon him) said: "Every deed of the son of Adam will be multiplied between ten and seven hundred times. Allah, may He be glorified and exalted, said: Except fasting. It is for Me and I shall reward for it. He gives up his desires and his food for My sake."

Narrated by Muslim (1151)

Fasting in the month or in any other month works as a shield in the day of judgement. It can help one from the horrific Hell-fire.

"Fasting is a shield with which a servant protects himself from the Fire." [Ahmad. *Sahih*]

Ramadan is the month to prepare muslims for the entire year to live a life of salvation, spirituality, giving, charity, spreading peace. Each and every second of Ramadan is precious. It is a way to get connected with Allah.

"There are in the month of Ramadhan in every day and night those to whom Allah grants freedom from the Fire, and there is for every Muslim

an supplication which he can make and will be granted." [Al-Bazzar and Ahmad. *Sahih*]

It is also the month of paying Zakat (charity) which is another obligatory act in Islam.

14. Who is Dajjal?

Ad-Dajjal means lier or deceiver in English. He is also entitled as Al Maseeh (Al-Massiah). Muslims believer in the final Hour when the earth and everything in it would perish away within a blink of an eye. Before the Hour arrives, the arrival of Dajjal would occur.

Dajjal is known as Anti-Christ and according to Islamic believe it is Isa (AS)/Christ who would descend from the heaven and fight with Dajjal and subsequently defeat him. Before Christ arrives, ImaanShafi would be the one who would guide the Muslims.

Dajjal is blind from one eye. On his forehead there would be written "infidel ,, which in arabic is kafir. He is the ultimate deceiver, he would have immense food and property in both of his hands and the people remaining on earth would get lured by those property. When Dajjal would come, the earth would be facing faminine like it never faced before so naturally it would be easy for Dajjal to make people choose him over God.

Ibn Khuzaimah, and ad-Dhiyaa', attributed to Abu Umamah, reports that the Prophet of Allah, sallallahu 'alaihi wa sallam, said:

"There will be three hard years before the Dajjal (appears). During them, people will be stricken by a great famine. In the first year, Allah will command the sky to withhold a third of its rain, and the earth to withhold a third a third of its produce. In the second year, Allah will command the sky to withhold two thirds of its rain, and the earth to withhold two thirds of its produce. In the third year, Allah will command the sky to withhold all of its rain, and it will not rain a single drop of rain. He will command the earth to withhold all of its produce, and no plant will grow. All hoofed animals will perish, except that which Allah

wills." He (sallallahu `alaihi wa sallam) was asked, 'What sustains people during that time?' He said, "Tahlil, takbir and tahmid (Saying, la ilaha ill Allah, Allahu Akbar and alhamdulillah). This will sustain them just as food does."

[Sahih Al-Jami` as-Saghir, no. 7875]

He would claim that he is God. He would even promise to bring back the death, but in reality he would only do magic which would show a mirrage of the death. It is Isa (As)/Jesus/Christ who would defeat the ferocious beast and bring back peace in the face of the earth.

15. Is Hijab only obligatory for women?

Hijab means veil and it is usually ascribed to veiling of the hair, neck and chest for women. Muslim women wear hijab to protect themselves and so that non-muslims can know detect them as muslims and keep away from them.

But the lesser known fact is hijab is not just covering your head, but it is an act of worshipping Allah. With Hijab you also need to wear clothes that are not tight fitted so that your body shape does not get revealed. You cannot wear transparent clothes. Another lesser known fact is Hijab also applies to men. It is in their eyes, meaning men cannot stare at a woman shamelessly. Only the first glance is permitted, after that they should lower their gaze. Women should cover themselves to protect themselves and men should also lower their gaze to protect themselves from turbulence.

It is incumbent upon a man to avert his gaze from looking at women; Allaah, Most High says:

Tell the believing men to lower their gaze (from looking at forbidden things), and protect their private parts (from illegal sexual acts). That is purer for them. Verily, Allaah is All-Aware of what they do. [An-Nur 24:30]

In the Quran there is a verse,

O Prophet, tell your wives and your daughters and the women of the believers to bring down over themselves [part] of their outer garments. That is more suitable that they will be known and not be abused. And ever is Allah Forgiving and Merciful.

"This is more appropriate so that they may be known [as Muslim women] and thus not be harassed [or molested]."

[Surah 33 Verse 59]

Hijab helps women to work on their inner beauty and not be in the vanity race of proving who is more beautiful. Hijab lets women and men define their own beauty. Beauty always fades, it is the inside of a person that counts and hijab lets you practice that.

16. What is the place of women in Islam?

In today's world there is constant news about girl child killing, girl child abortioning, wife beating and forced marriages and although these things occured and still occuring among non-muslims too, but people tend to ascribe Islam with mistreatment of women.

If you look at the Hadiths and Quranic Verses in Islam you would be shocked how high women are placed in Islam.

In Muhammad's (PBUH) lifetime he always showed mercy to all his wives and daughters. Despite having a mission to spread Islam all through the world, he used to spend quality time with his wives and daughters. There are numerous references where he was seen showing compassion towards them.

Women are definitely a blessing in Islam.

"He (God) it is who did create you from a single soul and therefrom did create his mate, that he might dwell with her (in love)..." **[Noble Quran 7:189]**

Women are given rights just like men. Their rights may be slightly different but nontheless they were given proper rights.

"...And they (women) have rights similar to those (of men) over them, and men are a degree above them." **[Noble Quran 2:228]**

17. Is forced marriage allowed in Islam?

It is very much prevailing in the world that Islam clogs people with restrictions like forcedfully covering themselves, forcefully marrying their daughters and beating them up if they do not listen.

True Islam does not support oppression. In Islam nothing is forced upon anyone. Islam is the religion of peace and it evokes peaceful coexistence of dissimilarities. Islam does encourage and finds it fundamental to spread the knowledge of Islam, but there is a fine line between spreading the knowledge and forcefully trying to make people accept it.

Forced marriage in Islam is not at all allowed. Any parents who forcefully marries off their daughters and sons would be answerable to Allah. The marriage itself would not be valid if the boy or the girl do not have their consent in it.

18. Is killing of a non-believer for the sake of spreading Islam allowed in Islam?

This is perhaps the most prevalent question that streams off any non-muslim's mind. Often times non-muslim may think "how can Islam be a religion of peace when numerous people are getting killed by Muslim extremists!" Fact of the matter is Islam does not allow any killing of innocent souls unless there is an absolute requirement. Spreading Islam does not require any bloodshed unless the non-believers declare a war against them.

A Muslim can spread the message of Allah and it is upon the non-believer whether they would accept the invitation or deny it. It is in no way in a Muslim's hand to decide who would join Islam and who would reject. Humans do not have the power to turn hearts, it is Allah's decree.

It is mentioned in the Quran that if a man is not kind to mankind, Allah would also not be kind to them. (here "mankind" refers to every human being, not just Muslims)

Narrated Jarir bin 'Abdullah: Allah's Apostle said, "Allah will not be merciful to those who are not merciful to mankind."

19. What are some intriguing and illustrative cases such as fatwas for teaching isalmic law?

Fatwa translates as legal opinion. In islam people rely on fatwa to go by their daily lives. The Quran and book of Hadiths are the guidance for the entire Muslim community but the hadiths are so vast that often times muslims are unable to read the entire collection of hadiths. For them who cannot study them on their own, they have to go towards certified jurist. In islam qualified jurists are called Mufti.

The fatwa is divided in 5 different sectors,

1. Obligatory
2. Commendable
3. Permissible
4. Despised
5. Not Permitted

There were some issues in the modern days that were not found in the days of prophets, Mufti's come to rescue with their knowledge of Quran and Shariah and offer solutions.

The fatwas can be on anything, from not being able to decide whether you can take your two year old to Hajj, whether to do a bank job, whether to watch Tv or listen to Music etc.

20. What is a list of isalmic-compliant companies in which I can buy shares as a beginner?

In islam taking interest (usury) is a sin and in fact considered as one of the major sins which would not be forgiven by God. Share business is permitted in Islam as long as you do not invest in companies that supports usury and are doing usury first hand.

There are numerous companies world wide that are running their business with the Islamic Shariah law. You can buy shares from them without worrying about comitting a major sin.

21. What are the best books to read learn about islam and Islamic culture?

The best book to learn about Islam is the Holy book of Quran, there is no substitute for it. As mentioned earlier, it is the spoken words of God and nothing can be compared with it. But the Quran does not elaborate on things, it only mentions the issues and gives the path and how would you get to that path needs to read from the deconstruction of Quran. There are many books that explain what each verse in the Quran mean, why they were revealed and upon which context they are applied to. Not every verse is applied in every single condition and quranic verse should be read as a whole chapter/surah and not taking out one single verse because it can mislead people sometimes.

Below is a list of books that would be wonderful as a starter to know about Islam. Some of the books are hyperlinked, so you can directly go to the source and get it from there.

Dua Weapon of the Believers by Yasir Qadhi

Reclaim Your Heart by Yasmin Mogahed

15 Ways to Increase Your Earnings from the Quran and Sunnah by *Yasir Qadhi*.

God, Islam &The Skeptic Mind: A Study on Faith, Science, Religious Diversity, Ethics and Evil

Worship Shelf (On Living Islam & Boosting Eeman)

"The Declaration of Faith" by *Shaykh Saalih ibn Fawzaan al-Fawzaan*.

Youth's problems by *Sheikh Muhammad Saalih Al-Uthaymeen*

Peace and conflict resolution in Islam by *Abdul Fatah Bello*

A Brief Illustrated Guide to Understanding Islam by *I.A Ibrahim*

Enjoy your life by *Dr. Muhammad 'Abd Rahman Al-'Arifi*

Psychology from The Islamic Perspective by *Dr. Aisha Utz*

Loving our Parents: Stories of duties and obligations by *Abdul Malik Mujahid*

The Muslim Family – The Marriage Series – Muhammad al-Jibaly

The Sealed Nectar (Ar Raheeq Al Makhtoom) by *Safiur Rahman Mubarakpuri*

Men & Women around the Messenger (saw) by *Khaalid Muhammad Khalid and Dr. Abdel-Hamid Eliwa*

From My Sisters' Lips by *Naima. B. Roberts* (personal narratives of other reverts to Islam)

Although, Islamic culture varies from countries to countries but the essential belief is same everywhere. In Egypt you may see people dressing up differently and in Saudi Arabia or Malaysia there are different attires too. But the fundamental issues in Islam do not change depending on the place.

22. How should I start engaging in islam?

To engage in Islam first you need to know what is Islam. We have already discussed it in our earlier questions. Without knowing what is Islam, what are the essential belief that Islam is build upon, what is the purpose of Islam, how would it benefit you and the rest of the humanity etc you cannot engage fruitfully in Islam.

Allah makes it much easier for anyone who wants to explore Islam, if you take one step towards Islam, Allah would open up several opportunities for you to explore more. Allah your creator gave you a well functioning brain, use it wisely and explore. Read a lot and try to reason with the facts. Islam does not invoke anyone to follow it blindly nor does it say we have to become an extremist about it.

Here is an effective hadith how Allah's image should be in our vision and how he thinks of us.

*The Prophet (peace be upon him) related to us that Allah says: "I am as My servant thinks of Me. I am with him when he remembers Me. If he mentions Me within himself, I mention him within Myself. If he mentions Me in an assembly, I mention him in a better assembly. If he comes near to Me a handspan, I come near to him the distance of a cubit. If he comes near to Me the distance of a cubit, I come near to him the distance of two outspread arms. If he comes to Me walking, I come to him running." [*Sahîh al-Bukhârî*(6856) and* Sahîh Muslim *(4832)]*

Al-Hasan al-Basrî said: "The believer assumes the best about his Lord so he does the best deeds. The sinner assumes the worst about his Lord, so he does evil deeds."

Is islam misogynistic?

I have already cleared how women are seen in Islam, so I would not repeat myself. Islam is in no way misogynistic. Below are some proofs from the Quran and hadiths.

It was explained by Muhammad (PBUH) that the best of men are those who are best to their wives.

The mother of a child is so respected in Islam that it is reported that she has 3 times more rights above the child than the father.

"O Messenger of Allah! Who is most deserving of my fine treatment?" He (ﷺ) said, "Your mother, then your mother, then your mother, then your father, then your nearest, then nearest". [Al-Bukhari and Muslim].

It is adviced to men to be kind to their wives.

The holy Quran states: *"...But consort with them in kindness, for if you hate them it may happen that you hate a thing wherein God has placed much good."* (4: 19).

In islam when marrages take place, men have to give their wives a wedding gift which is also known as Mahr in arabic. The women are in charge of deciding how much mahr they should be getting. This shows how well treated women are in Islam.

There are also other narrations that show beating your wife mercilessly is not Islamic.

Narrated 'Abdullah bin Zam'a: The Prophet said, *"None of you should flog his wife as he flogs a slave and then have sexual intercourse with her in the last part of the day." [Hadith 132]*

23. Should americans fear islam?

Americans like most western countries exclusively fear Islam because of the numerous extremist groups like Taleban, Isis, Al-Qaeda etc. These groups in the name of spreading Islam does horrible deeds like suicide bombing, bombing, sun shooting and stabbing someone to death.

After the 9/11 incident, every one is quite fearful of Islam. But if you take a look at the Islamic teachings and laws if you find that Islam does not promote any violence. It gives you the best teachings to beautify this life and the afterlife. It gives you a purpose to live and something to strife for. Without having casue to live, is there any value of that life? And if you consider having a good degree, a well paid job and a family is the cause of life, what happens when you attain all of that? Does your life come to an end? Islam gives you a purpose to earn God's mercy and be eternally in peace in the afterlife.

Islam does give commandments to spread the message of Allah and His oneness but it does not want to cause fright in people. Of course you must fear the one who created you, but that fear should not supercede your love for your creator. If you go in a zoo and suddenly found out a lion has escaped its cage and it is 100 feet away from you, wouldn't you be naturally scared? So what about the creator who created you, the lion and anything in this universe? Shouldn't He deserve your utmost reverence?

Fearing Allah in a way that He can give you everything and take everything from you in a blink of eye is encouraged but you should never fear Islam.

24. Is islam political?

Politics in the dictionary means "Social relations involving intrigue to gain authority or power,, and political in the dictionary means "Of or relating to your views about social relationships involving authority or power,,. Both the meaning involves power and authority and Islam does not want to gain any authority in the world. As I have already mentioned quite few times that Allah the supreme does not need us, our worldly goods, our property but it is us who are in need of Allah's mercy. Islam is there to show us the righteous path and by establishing Islam in the face of the earth cannot make or break the God. He was supreme and He would still be the governing power over the universe even if one single Muslim is not alive in the world.

Unlike politics, Islam does not favour one party over the another. It serves equally to everyone living anyweher in the world. Depending on someone's social status, property and earnings Islam does not change its ruling. Itis same for the poor and the rich.

25. Is the behavior of isis representative of the religion of islam?

First things first, let know what is Isis. Its acronym is Islamic State of Syria and Iraq. The roots were first traces back in 2003. Later on it grew and now it seems to be the number one terror striking group of extremist that ever walked on earth with the label that they are spreading Islam.

It is ironic because real Islam is not about violence, causing terror and killing of innocent lives. Islam never wanted bloodshed unless a war was raised against the Muslims directly.

According to a 2008 propaganda video released by the group, the purpose of ISIS is to serve as a "dagger in the American-Jewish plan for the region ... The establishment of the Islamic State ... is the gate through which the conquest of Jerusalem will be achieved and the filth of the Jewish thieves will be removed from the heart of the Islamic world."

If God wanted to vanish the Jew from the face of this earth, He could have done that way back in Hitler's time. God gave them a chance to revert back to the righteous path. It is only God who is apt to punish the sinful and Islam does not allow raising terror in order to convert people to Islam.

Isis is not even trying to convert the non-believers to Islam, they are simply vanishing them away and thinking this is the right way to establish Islam. Sadly enough there are thousands of Muslims who do not perform the fundamentals of Islam and still breathing on this earth. Islam is something very individual and how one person would practice Islam is entirely in their hands. Whether a Muslim Lady would cover their faces or not, none can force it upon her. It is her discretion and if she is in the right path she would get its reward from God and vice versa.

Isis also deforms the body of their victims, which is completely prohibited in Islam.

Further more if someone kills an innocent soup without any proper reason, he would not die as a Muslim. So Isis's claim to fight for Islam is quite vein.

Imam (a.s.) further says:

"One who kills a believer intentionally is deprived of the 'Tawfiq' of repenting (for his sins)."

26. What caused the rise of Islamic extremism?

Wherever there is a despair, anarchy and extremism, be it in any community, nation it is due to misguidance. When people take things too seriously and become oblivious of any other interpretations other than theirs, it is then they make the gravest sins.

The Islamic extremist groups too are perhaps misguided, misleaded and blindly following the path of astray. Satan is the number one emeny of Mankind and perhaps it is Satan who is deceiving them in the name of Islam. Satan can only give ideas to men, it is men who actually performs the task and if a man is strong in his belief of Allah and His teachings, he would never be deceived by false ideas.

In the Quran there are several indications that encourage a peaceful existing of the believers and non-believers yet they choose to ignore it.

"And whoever kills a believer intentionally, his punishment is Hell; he shall abide in it, and Allah will send His wrath on him and curse him and prepare for him a painful chastisement." (Surah an-Nisā' 4:93)

It is clear in the above verse that the ultimate punishment of killing an innocent soul would be invaribly HELL.

"Nor take life -- which Allah has made sacred -- except for just cause. And if anyone is slain wrongfully, we have given his heir authority (to demand retaliation or to forgive): but let him not exceed bounds in the matter of taking life, for he is helped (by the Law)." [Quran 17:33]

"Permission (to fight) is given to those upon whom war is made because they are oppressed, and most surely Allah is well able to assist them." [Quran 22: 39]

In the Hadith below it is evident that Islam does not want extremism, and that is why it is discouraging killing children and women in war.

Narrated 'Abdullaah, may Allah be pleased with him: "During some of the battles of the Prophet ﷺ a woman was found killed. Allah's Apostle disapproved the killing of women and children." [Al-Bukhari]

27. Is the spread of islam dangerous?

How can a religion be dangerous when all it wants is to show the righteous path and guide men to be successful not in just this world but also in the hereafter! The Holy book's message is Peace and this is what is prevailing all through the book.

It encourages one to forgive and remain patience. It teaches people to be kind to one another even if they are your enemy. Forgiving your friends is sometime tough, can you imagine forgiving your enemy? But if you believe in the hereafter and its promises, you would forgive and forget.

"And there is life for you in (the law of) retaliation, O people of understanding, that you may guard yourselves."[Quran 2:179]

It teaches people to take care of your parents, to stay away from fornication, adultery. It teaches people to remain patient even when you lose your dear ones to death. It teaches people to control their anger.

"The recompense for an injury is an injury equal thereto (in degree): but if a person forgives and makes reconciliation, his reward is due from Allah: for (Allah) loves not those who do wrong. But indeed if any do help and defend themselves after a wrong (done) to them, against such there is no cause of blame. The blame is only against those who oppress men and insolently transgress beyond bounds through the land, defying right and justice: for such there will be a grievous penalty. And whoever is patient and forgiving, these most surely are actions due to courage." [Quran 42:40-43]

Islam teaches people to keep faith in God and the mercy of God. Here there is a good lesson of remaining calm in desperate hour.

Allah says, conveying to us the words of his prophet Jacob (peace be upon him): "Never despair of Allah's mercy. No one despairs of Allah's mercy except the unbelieving people." [Sûrah Yûsuf: 87]

28. How is life for a hindu woman converted to islam?

Life of a Hindu woman would be quite the same as it would be for an atheist, Christian, Buddist or Jew if they were to convert to Islam. In Islam if a non-believer converts to Islam, from then their every sin is forgiven by Allah.

If a practising Hindu woman converts to Islam, they would be already accustomed to worshipping Gods, but in Islam she would have to learn that Allah is one and He has no lineage. She have to accept the pillars of Islam, that is Praying, Fasting in the month of Ramadan, Zakat, Pilgrimage (If she is financially sufficient).

She would also have to protect her by covering herself according to the Islamic law. In Hindu marriages the bride have to pay dowry, but in Islamic marriage she would be the one who would receive a wedding gift (the sum of which she would decide).

29. What are the advantages of converting to islam from Christianity?

In Christianity, people believe that Prophet Isa (AS)/Jesus/Christ is the son of God and they follow the book Bible/Injeel. But in Islam people believe after Isa (AS), the last and final prophet came to this earth, namely Muhammad (PBUH) with the Holy Book of Quran.

When Quran was revealed, the book Bible/Injeel was ousted. The Christian must take Shahada and say, Allah is one and Muhammad (PBUH) is His last messenger.

The advantages of converting would be having their sins removed completely. Allah would not ask about anything of his life before he converted to Islam and he would only be accounted for the things he does after the convertion to Islam. This could be the greatest gift a anyone can ever have.

A man called Amr came to the Prophet Muhammad and said, "Give me your right hand so that I may give you my pledge of loyalty." The Prophet stretched out his right hand. Amr withdrew his hand. The Prophet said: {What has happened to you, O Amr?} He replied, "I intend to lay down a condition." The Prophet asked: {What condition do you intend to put forward?} Amr said, "That God forgive my sins." The Prophet (PBUH) said:

{Didn't you know that converting to Islam erases all previous sins? [Sahih Muslim -121]

It does not stop there, Allah would also make the first few months or a year of the convertion to Islam really easy. Every prayer he would pray, every good deed he would perform, he would be very satisfied with it.

30. Is nationalism un-islamic?

Nationalism from the dictionary meaning means "Love of country and willingness to sacrifice for it,, or "The doctrine that your national culture and interests are superior to any other,,. There are couple of other meanings too, but more or less they are the same as mentioned above. Now if we look at the first definition, no one can object to it as sacrificing oneself for the sake of their country cannot be a bad thing. But if we add a search light to the second definition, it clearly implies "I'm better than you,, ideology. A sort of boasting is there and Islam does not encourgae in fact it discourages people to boast upon anything they have be it their physical appearance, their earthly belongings or their nation.

Another important factor is Islam sees the entire mankind as one single Ummah of Muhammad (PBUH) and everyone despite their cultural difference, their skin tone and their respective individual values, the single thread of Islam should combine them all. There should be no feeling of superiority in regards to the current condition of their nation.

When you want to scarifice to protect your nation, that is not un-islamic but when you boast over your nation and feel superior over other nations, this is definitely an un-islamic act. Also extremism is strictly frowned upon in Islam and nationalism should not cross the boundary.

In todays world most of the countries are facing wars because of extreme nationalist mentality.

31. How did it feel to leave islam?

Often times people who do not really understand Islam leaves Islam at some point of there life. The 5 pillars of Islam for instance, other than the daily prayers and the belief in Allah's oneness, the rest of fasting, Charity and Hajj are suppose be done in a special time of the year. But some people find the pressure of the 5 daily prayers too much. It is mostly because they haste in their prayers. They see it as a burden and the sooner they can finish it, they feel it is better! But when you haste in your prayers, the sweetness of the prayer dissappears. A true Muslim who is in the righteous path gets the most from the daily prayers, they sit for sufficient time in each prayer and ask Allah for whatever they need. Even if their prayers are not answered right away, they feel relieved because it works as a therapy.

There is also a pressure of staying away from certain things like not being able to beautify oneself in front of others, not being able to indulge in fornication, not being able to lie, cheat, have usury, covering your body parts etc. It gets tough on Muslims if they in their mind find Islamic law as as a burden. So, for x,y,z reason when they leave Islam, initially they feel FREE.

But after a certain point they feel void inside, they have no eternal casue to live for. They have only worldly goals and when failure comes down upon them they feel completely helpless. There is no soothing factor left for them. Earlier they could always say their prayers, cry to God and wear off the burden. After leaving Islam life initially seems free but later on absolute void takes over their heart.

32. Is islam a race?

Race is "People who are believed to belong to the same genetic stock,, and No Islam is not a race. Islam does not care if you are Asian, African, American, Arabian, Lebenese, Philipo or Indian. Islam does not care if you are a minority. Islam is for everyone and it is applied to everyone. Every one is born as Muslims, it is later on they discover their parents have certain beliefs and those beliefs are tharshed upon them. Allah single handedly created all and therefore everyone is born as a Muslim.

Islam is a way of life for everyone. Just because you were born in a Christian family or Jewish family does not mean you would be not be answerable to God after death. Every soul shall taste death and every soul has to answer to his lord for the activities in the world when the time comes.

33. What distinguishes islam from Islamism?

Islam is a way of peaceful life in this world and the hereafter. Whereas Islamism is a way to convert every single being into Muslim whether by hook or by crock. Islam is founded upon FAITH but Islamism is founded upon IDEOLOGY.

When you take pure Islam as your guide, you would listen to the words of Allah that is written in the Quran and try to follow it as much as you can without harming anyone else. Islam does not ask you to play the Godfather of this world and decide who should live and who should die! Islamism is taking the essentials of Islamic law and try to rule the world with it even if the receiver is declined towards it.

Allah never asked humans to go to extreme ends to convert someone into being a Muslim. It is their own will and none but the person himself and Allah can make them convert. Islamism is the extremist form of Islam which is not at all encouraged in Islam.

34. Is islam good or bad?

The question is very valid considering the numerous terrorist groups that are prevalent all over the world. Recently Isis is making news almost every day and everyone is driving further away from Islam because of those groups.

Any one or any group who take Islam as means to justify their wrong doings, killing is not a Muslim at all and he would not die as a Muslim either. Again the issue of Islam and Islamism comes ahead. We cannot look at certain people and their evil deeds and think this is what Islam represents because what they are practicing is no way near to what true Islam preaches.

Islam does not want anarchy among people, community or nation. Islam wants harmony and have given the guidance to keep that harmony. Even during the time of Muhammad (PBUH) and his companions, there Hindus, Atheist and Jews lived their respective lives without harming each other.

Now you need to ask yourself if a religion that promotes harmony, prohibits sinful acts like lying, cheating, backbiting, killing without any cause, fornicating, adultery, jealousy and greed can be bad?

35. Is islam and islamization a threat to india and hindus?

Islam is not a threat to anyone as long as they do not start a war against the Muslims. If a war is declared against them, it is obvious that they would have to fight regardless. The most growing religion in todays age is Islam and it is causing a terror in the skeptic minds. To be honest, you only fear a thing when you do not know about it clearly. If you know what Islam stands for, there is no reason run away from it let alone fear it!

Islamization is not a treat to India, America or any other country. Likely it is not a treat to the Hindus, Christians, Jews etc. Recently a Hindu man was beaten by Muslims in Pakistan for eating in a restuarant around the time of fasting! This is outrageous and Islam does not ask any Muslim to do this. In fact those who have beaten that man up would be hold accounted for this terrible act.

Few days ago, In India a man was beaten to death because he was suspected to eat beef which is currently not allowed to consume by the Indian Government. This is another act of extremism and I'm sure Hinduism does not encourage it either. In India now a law is prevailing that cows cannot slaughter cows as a sacrifice in Muslim's religious festive, Eid Al Azha because Hindus consider cow as a deity. That is understandable as it is basically a Hindu country but beating someone to death for it is in no way understandable.

Just like Muslims cannot break a temple because it upholds contrary to their belief, similarly Hindus cannot break a Mosque. There should be a peaceful co-existing environment where no one is threaten by the other party.

36. Is there such a thing as moderate islam?

If you look at the dictionary meaning MODERATE it means "Being within reasonable or average limits; not excessive or extreme ,,.

Now from the surface level it seems quite reasonable definition and any ideology and belief should not cross limits and become extreme in its nature. Extremism frowned upon in Islam and it is adviced not to cross limits.

Having said that if a person in terms of being within limits leaves one of the 5 daily prayers, that would definitely not be allowed. It would be considered a sin and he would be held for it in the day of judgement.

If a person lives in a summer country and find it rather difficult to cover their body according to the Islamic law, and dresses as like as they please, that moderation would not be allowed in Islam. You cannot leave the fundamentals of Islam in order to remain a moderate Muslim. You have to maintain the obligatory things and then regarding the voluntery things you can remain moderate.

37. Is islam a religion of peace?

From the above 36 question answered, with several references from the Quran and Sunnah (Hadith) of Muhammad (PBUH), it is without any doubt that Islam is a religion of PEACE. Every where in the Quran Allah talked about salvation and peace. Following are few verses on peace from the Holy Quran.

"O You who believe! Enter absolutely into peace (Islam). Do not follow in the footsteps of satan. He is an outright enemy to you." (Surah al-Baqara Verse 2: 208)

"God does not forbid you from being good to those who have not fought you in the religion or driven you from your homes, or from being just towards them. God loves those who are just." (Surat al-Mumtahana, 8)

"God does not love corruption". (Surat al-Baqara, verse 205)

38. Is music prohibited in islam? Why?

There is awide debate surrounding the issue of music in Islam, mostly because there is no clear prohibition in Quran regarding music. But there are several hadiths that mention music is frowned upon in Islam. It has reasons behind it of course.

Anyone who listens to music at some point of their life they become addicted to it. They listen to music all the time. If they are writing an article, doing office work at home, doing math, solving a puzzle, sometimes even eating, they must have music playing in the background in order for them to focus. They need to sooth their mind and soul with music before they can focus on anything. This is a PROBLEM because Islam does not want humans to be slaves to their addiction.

Another important thing regarding music is it takes the human away from God and devine spirituality and focus it in the worldly affairs. There are good effects of music on the mind too, like music therapy. But the bad in it supercedes the good. It intoxicates the mind and soul and the consumers of music find it unnecessary to work on the path of God anymore. It basically diverts their mind.

There are several hadiths on the music instruments being frowned upon in Islam.

*Narrated Abu Amir or Abu Malik Al Ashari that he heard the Prophet saying, "From among my followers there will be some people who will consider illegal sexual intercourse, the wearing of silk, the drinking of alcoholic drinks and the use of **musical instruments**, as lawful. And there will be some people who will stay near the side of a mountain and in the evening their shepherd will come to them with their sheep and ask them for something, but they will say to him, 'Return to us tomorrow.'*

Allah will destroy them during the night and will let the mountain fall on them, and He will transform the rest of them into monkeys and pigs and they will remain so till the Day of Resurrection." [Sahih Al-Bukhari Vol.7 Hadith No.5590]

One instrument that was evidently found permitted is DAFF (tambourine).

Narrated Urwa on the authority of Aisha

"On the days of Mina, (11th, 12th, and 13th of Dhul-Hijjah) Abu Bakr came to her while two young girls were beating the tambourine (daff) and the Prophet was lying covered with his clothes. Abu Bakr scolded them. The Prophet uncovered his face and said to Abu Bakr, "Leave them, for these days are the days of 'Id and the days of Mina." [Sahih Al-Bukhari Vol.2 Hadith No.987]

There is a really good book that you can read to make your understanding regarding music in Islam more clear.

The Music Made Me Do It: An In-Depth study of Music through Islam and Science by *Dr. Gohar Mushtaq.*

39. Is islam a religion that somehow makes some proportions of its followers the most violent people on earth?

This accusation comes from the numerous activities that is prevailing all over the world that makes people question a Peaceful religion like Islam.

Whenever there is a person doing an evil deed, he always tries to justify with a good excuse. This excuse works as or supposed to work as a shield for him. But in reality no matter how hungry a person may be stealing is never justified for him. No matter how sad or desperate a person may be, suicide is never justified.

Similarly the violent people who walk on earth holding the sign of Islam and tell the world they are trying to establish peace by casuing a little bit anarchy is another shield that supposed to justify their horrible acts.

Islam preaches kindness, humility, and anyone who is not kind towards all creature not just human, God is disappointed on them.

Islam does not encourage anyone to be violent regardless of the context. Rather it discouranges being outrageous and boastfulness.

According to a tradition recorded in the Sahih of Imam Muslim, when the Prophet's opponents greatly increased their persecution, his Companions asked him to curse them. At this the Prophet replied, "I have not been sent to lay a curse upon men but to be a blessing to them." His opponents continued to treat him and his Companions unjustly and cruelly, but he always prayed for them.

Printed in Great Britain
by Amazon